German children's book:

My Daddy is the Best!

Mein Papa ist der Beste!

Translation:
Dr. Nicolle Kränkel

Sujatha Lalgudi

Ted and Tia are making a card for daddy.
They wonder what to write on the card.

Ted und Tia basteln Glückwunschkarten für ihren Vater.
Sie fragen sich, was sie auf die Karten schreiben sollen.

Suddenly Ted shouts, all excited. "I know, I know...

Plötzlich ruft Ted ganz aufgeregt: "Ich weiß es, ich weiß es:

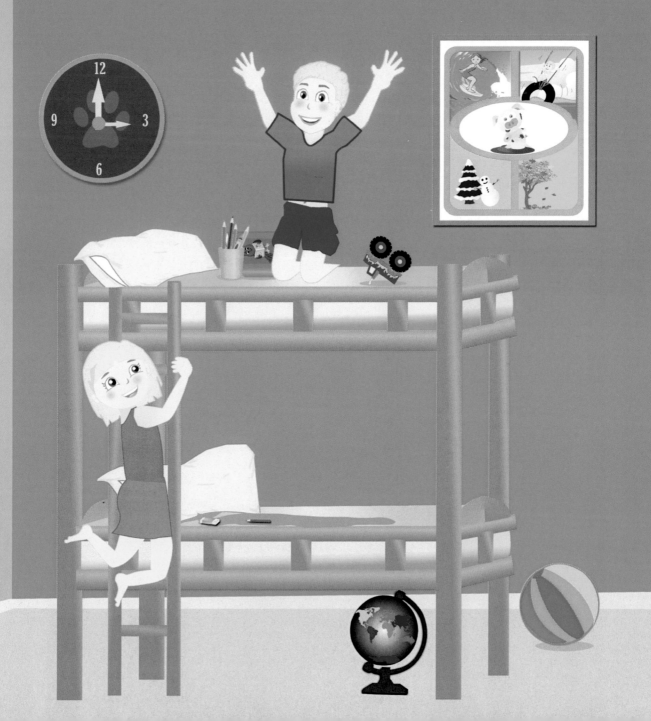

Daddy makes the best BBQ when we go camping."

Papa grillt die besten Würstchen, wenn wir zelten fahren."

"I love Dad because he makes me laugh when I am sad." Tia beams.
"He throws me up in the sky."

"Ich mag Papa, weil er mich zum Lachen bringt, wenn ich traurig bin." sagt Tia.
"Er wirft mich hoch in den Himmel."

"Daddy pushes me high on the swing."

"Papa schiebt mich an, wenn ich schaukle."

Ted remembers Daddy cheering him at his baseball games. A smile crosses his face.

Ted erinnert sich, dass Papa ihm beim Baseball zugejubelt hat. Er lächelt, als er daran denkt.

"He made a bed for poor birdie with the broken wing", says Tia.

"Er hat ein Bett gebaut, für den Vogel mit dem gebrochenen Flügel." sagt Tia.

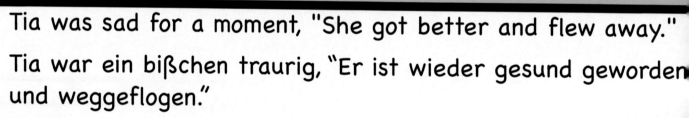

Tia was sad for a moment, "She got better and flew away."

Tia war ein bißchen traurig, "Er ist wieder gesund geworden und weggeflogen."

They remember their fun day at the Fair.
"I loved the airplane ride!", says Tia.

Sie erinnern sich an den Tag auf der
Kirmes.
"Das Flugzeug war toll!", sagt Tia.

"I loved the bumper-car ride!"

"Ich fand den Autoscooter am besten!"

Ted loved seeing the Clown juggling pins while riding a unicycle.

Der Clown war lustig! Er konnte Einrad fahren und gleichzeitig jonglieren.

"He carries me when I am too tired to walk anymore."

"Er trägt mich, wenn ich nicht mehr laufen kann."

"He is the best monster", exclaims Ted.

"Er ist das beste Monster", ruft Ted.

together?"

"Erinnerst du dich an die Filme, die wir zusammen angeschaut haben?"

Ted sometimes loves the popcorn more than the movie.

Ted mag manchmal das Popcorn lieber als den Film.

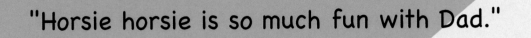

"Horsie horsie is so much fun with Dad."

"Hoppe-Hoppe-Reiter macht so viel Spass
mit Papa."

"Best of all, I love the way he reads bedtime stories and tucks me in bed."

"Am meisten mag ich, wenn er mich abends ins Bett bringt und mir Geschichten vorliest."

"Don't forget the pillow fights", adds Tia.

"Vergiss nicht die Kissenschlacht!" fügt Tia hinzu.

"We have the best dad in the world."
Tia's card reads,"You are the best dad, Daddy,
Your little Princess."

"Wir haben den besten Papa auf der Welt!"
Auf Tia's Karte steht: "Du bist der beste
Papa. Deine kleine Prinzessin"

Ted card says, "You are my super hero, signed, Super Boy."

Auf Ted's Karte steht: "Du bist mein Superheld. Dein Super-Boy".

Ted hugs daddy.

Ted umarmt Papa.

Tia gives a kiss to daddy.

Tia gibt ihm einen Kuss.

They say together, "You are the best daddy in the world. We love you".

Zusammen sagen sie: "Du bist der beste Papa auf der Welt.
Wir haben dich ganz doll lieb!"

Daddy smiles and says softly to Grandpa,
"You are the best dad, Father".

Papa lächelt und sagt zum Großvater:
"Du bist der beste Papa, Vater."

Thank you!
Happy Father's Day!

Vielen Dank!
Alles Gute zum Vatertag!

Made in the USA
Las Vegas, NV
10 February 2021